IMPROVISED EXPLOSIVE DEVICE

Arji Manuelpillai is a poet, performer and creative facilitator based in London. His poetry has appeared in magazines including *Poetry Wales*, *The Rialto* and *bath magg*, and his debut pamphlet, *Mutton Rolls*, was published with Out-Spoken Press. Arji was shortlisted for the Oxford Prize, the Live Canon Prize, the National Poetry Prize and the Winchester Prize, and was runner-up in the Robert Graves Prize. He is a member of Malika's Poetry Kitchen and London Stanza, received an Arts Council England award to develop his creative practice, and worked with Hannah Lowe as part of the Jerwood/Arvon Mentoring Programme.

ALSO BY ARJI MANUELPILLAI

Mutton Rolls (Out-Spoken Press, 2020)

Improvised Explosive Device

ARJI MANUELPILLAI

Penned in the Margins

LONDON

PUBLISHED BY PENNED IN THE MARGINS
Toynbee Studios, 28 Commercial Street, London E1 6AB
www.pennedinthemargins.co.uk

First published 2022

Printed in the United Kingdom by TJ Books Limited

ISBN
978-1-913850-08-1

CONTENTS

Improvised
Explosive
Device

'Consider the subtleness of the sea; how its most dreaded creatures glide under water, unapparent for the most part, and treacherously hidden beneath the loveliest tints of azure. Consider also the devilish brilliance and beauty of many of its most remorseless tribes, as the dainty embellished shape of many species of sharks. Consider, once more, the universal cannibalism of the sea; all whose creatures prey upon each other, carrying on eternal war since the world began.

Consider all this; and then turn to this green, gentle, and most docile earth; consider them both, the sea and the land; and do you not find a strange analogy to something in yourself?'

Herman Melville, MOBY-DICK; OR, THE WHALE (1851)

watch it swim
down into the
marrow of us
down so we
raise our heads
our chins kiss
the ceiling
gasping like
blood bags

the city's full
of broken doors
routine searches
putting a
proverbial
hand around
our proverbial
neck and telling
ourselves to
speak our truth

there is nothing
anyone can do
but watch
a teen roughed-
up walking
from school

when they ask
you where it
all began you
will say you
have no idea

Portrait of a Man Fitting into a Fake Suicide Vest

This story is a star shooting dead across the sky —
a cliché, I know, but by the time you see a man

slide polystyrene into the pockets of a vest
he is already dead. By the time the journalist

sees *maniac* trending, a jaw's swiped left.
It should feel snug, almost impossible to remove

the political from a message of condolence,
from the two seats lying empty beside me.

A Tesco bag is shaken across the bedroom floor:
a route marked black, a maggot-pit of wires,

Sellotape, clips, a pair of red-handled scissors.
It wants to be below the arms, flush, like a carrier.

A reporter's up all night collating material to stitch
this story: a displaced family, high school dropout,

prison stint, Mujahideen, on tag, the packaging
spits pebbledash across the carpet, a snow globe

cracked in a tight fist. It has to seem realistic,
like he grew round the back of an army barracks,

listening to boots chug, the slow ease of velcro straps.
It should feel like an other's skin until this story's in bits

spread across a bedroom floor. In this light it could
be an office suit, an armoured vest, a life jacket.

Rapid Eye Movement

Slapping a newsfeed from a daydream, a hundred pointing fingers, pushed from cars, hung from balconies, shouting *bloody hell look at that fucking guy* and I am trying to write a text, *hey babes how was the* — but it snatches an iris, the phone lit by a man made lunatic, a blade like a toothpick in the stomach of a spider, a can of scarpering legs, the figure swinging his chest like his heart is trying to speak, *we interrupt this broadcast* — pixels lather hot from a van, officers pouring into the road, passers-by covering their eyes with holy hands, nails in teeth, phones up, trending: ATTACK, trending: Prayers For — *what I can say with certainty is that no one had the slightest inkling that he could or would do something like this* — all the while, that song, a man wrestled to concrete, a knee on the vocal cord, I cannot stop hearing that tune, the crack of jaw, the pop of rounds in the closed mouth of a man that looks so much like me, that tune, I have to stop texting my girlfriend, feeding off the live feed, marvel at the blood flowing into the snicks of the pavement. Listen, that song, *life, it's bigger than you and you are* — not this body tightening, reaching for meaning but where is the meaning in Michael Stipe writing a song on religion when really it's a song about love and loneliness?

He says it comes from an old Southern expression for being at the end of one's rope, but it can feel like a calling: being tugged at the end of one's rope.

The Mother

Everyone was far away enough to be so close to being
two handshakes away from a hand waving *hi mum I'm
on TV* a man is describing what happened

isn't what happened to a girl who saw the whole
thing walking into Pret for a toastie sharing the body
how it jerks like it left the house and forgot its keys

in the doorway of a block of flats a woman crumples
when she sees how lost her son was wandering furious
in the morning after her firstborn is shot dead twice

once by a bullet second by a neighbour shouting
KILLER scratched on a car disappears in her head
aches when she sees her boy in the newspaper barely

man oh man her knees buckle soft into the holes
in his face look how they made a monster
of her baby shifts cold as steel under mortuary

light still lives with a mother in his bedroom
exactly how he left it, there, on the edge of a bed
she rocks like a hook through the cheek of a fish.

Tusk

Passersby used Narwhal tusk & fire extinguisher to subdue attacker.
Such a British thing to do!
  @eastendenquirer

A scientist spots an oily blur below the ice: *Monodon monoceros.*
He tells an Inuit tale of a brave woman who harpooned a shadow,

how it pulled then dragged her body to the centre of the ocean.
The fisherman found her metamorphosed into the Great Narwhal,

topknot stiffened to a tusk, body ballooned into a Zeppelin,
singing those long sad ballads even as a hunter cuts her tusk out.

This perfect weapon — sold, hung and pulled from a wall and finally
smashed into the ribs of a stranger. This is what heroism looks like.

The policeman tells how the tusk is what feathers are to peacocks,
antlers to a stag, an empire to an island. After the photos,

the interviews, the tweets, the ex-girlfriend ringing out the blue,
the hero is pardoned for a murder he committed six years prior.

After the Prime Minister's Statement

At the local funfair
bags of goldfish
hang like organs.

My bros and I
jackpot coconuts,
choose a prize,

hold it to
the light to
catch scales

singing like
prison bars.
Those tiny spots,

my father says,
*that's how they
feel pressure.*

How do we know
when the air
is so dense

it could crack
a man's heart
clean through?

Open wide: sooner
you swallow,
sooner we can

get back to normal.
One time I haven't
shared with anyone:

I'm feeding Usman
(take it that's his name)
when I slip, honestly,

a whole can in,
and it falls like
confetti at a funeral.

I watch Usman
eat himself to death
and afterwards,

white as marble,
I tell my friends
he was depressed,

acting strangely,
nothing I could do.
No further comments

at this time.
It really is amazing
how a man can talk

without actually
saying anything.
I can't understand

what happened
between leaving
prison and waving

a knife like a flag.
They call it radicalised,
thought he was

de-radicalised,
but it turns out
there was something

in his eye.
To know a fish
well is to know

it's depressed.
It'll swim
to the top

of the tank
as though
trying to escape;

if you raise
the water level
higher, you'll find

it flapping
on the carpet
this way and that.

Mistaken Identity

Imagine an IC4
fits my description,
not jacked up tight
on a car bonnet,
legs spread like
a peace sign flipped.
That's me right now.
This IC4 is home
building bombs in
a damp flat in SE19.
This one wakes up
each day, bumbles
sleepy in cat slippers
and Christmas PJs
to a local shop
where a clerk
mistakenly thinks
he's a poet, *oh hi*,
each day, *aren't you
that poet*, each day,

I get that all the time.
Meanwhile police
are patting me down:
it'll only take a second.
One day he decides
to visit Foyles and
the cashier suggests
Dickman so
he reads it cover
to cover, likes it
so much he reads
it again and again.
He even begins
writing his own
poems — this one
you're reading now
is actually his —
and I am on my way
into the Oxford
Street Primark,
body puffed up
with C4.

188 to Greenwich

I'm weighing words on the bus just to pass the time.
Two women spar over an armrest. One says,

go back to your Chinese restaurant, and the bus jolts
like it's driven over a body. A Chinese

restaurant isn't a Chinese restaurant. It's a hard place
dropped from a nine-storey building. Somewhere

someone is finding a rock to crawl into.
When the other woman replies, *fuck off fat bitch*,

it feels by and by, prosaic, the bus rile up,
extending their phones like radiation specialists,

posting LIVE so it scatters as bullets from a sawn-off.
That night I cannot seem to shake it.

It deposits a dark spot somewhere in my body
like the spots of gum outside the train station.

I can't decide if it's what she did or what I didn't
but walking into a bar an old friend tells me

he isn't surprised: *hate crime is up by 108%.*
Suddenly I'm imagining all that chewing gum

deposited in the corners of our organs,
all that stickiness across our eyelids,

ears and teeth. On the bus on the way home
a white woman sits beside me. I have to fight

the urge to push her arm from the armrest.

Let's Just Call Them Butterflies

A boy, barely man, barely lucid, been barely outside in weeks,
hocked up in laptop light like a train's perpetually passing by.

A boy, barely man, nurturing an unhealthy obsession for
                butterflies —
the way the wings flicker like God is nudge nudge wink wink,

the way it's caterpillar-transformed, super slo-mo, saying, *look
I'm so delicately precious.* How quickly it veers to creating

a kind of chaos. Here are the facts: not in education or training,
problems making friends, socially awkward, the next video

will play in 5, 4, 3: you have to look for butterflies not in motion,
just sat there, delicate as stigma, sipping honeydew, nectar,

raise the net very slightly, no sudden movements and...
a hundred or so videos of butterflies being slammed on sills.

Each clip's a droplet of honey, each droplet curiously closer
to a pair of tweezers cold against a wing. Snap.

If you like what you see, click subscribe. Rare butterfly washes
up in Dover. Butterfly plague. The truth about butterflies.

Killing a butterfly is easy. It isn't long before he cannot stop
seeing it, there, in the space above the desk, dead,

the centrepiece of a bedroom. Framed.
Every morning he'll wake up and say, *I did it, I fucking got you.*

Methods of Fitting In

The neighbours next door are either having sex or arguing,
I can't tell which, just like I can't decide where to stand
when an anti-racist activist makes monkey noises at the EDL.
I'm on my third draft of a placard and it still feels judgey.
Meet Amrit, soldier at the Vali North torture camp, quiet chap,
tells me nobody knows themselves until they're pushed
to their absolute brink. It doesn't feel much like a placard,
but I imagine myself, hand on valve, edge of a Kalashnikov.
A few years back a black man was on the news talking inflation;
a good friend ripped a slur wide open like a packet of crisps.
I don't mean you though man, you've made an effort to blend in.
I could have been a poorly painted picture politely struck off kilter.
My aunty says: *survival is a matter of keeping a low profile.*

You Must Have Misheard Him

It's cumulative, a thread hanging from your favourite jumper, stop
going on about it catching the finger of some prick who pulls,
unravels you to blushing pink. Remember how you walked from
her house with morning hair and everyone was kissing and smiling
and laughing or in this case staring at you like you don't belong.
You really should have been in my skin, felt it plucked bare enough
to rip a fellow's larynx out. I'm so sorry no one understands
so I describe it as I do love, how you cannot stop thinking about them,
how it eats you up, that's what I'm trying to say, he wove an urchin
into the film of my iris, suddenly everything I see is him. I become
what liberals call 'white trash'. Not everything is about race until
something is about race, until you can't sleep without the TV on.

The Cameraman

In a nature documentary the film crew never gets involved.
An elephant they have been trailing for years is dragged

to death by a circle of hyenas.
On BBC News a brown man slumps to the pavement.

That night the cameraman cannot stop seeing it.
An expanding sinkhole appears beside his bed. Everything

is pulled, scraping like chairs across stainless steel floors. Look,
all we want is to belong, to feel we are not part of

the sound of flesh pulled from the jugular, so mesmerising.
We only want the animals to act as they would normally act,

as if we weren't even there. Sometimes if we're lucky,
they'll creep up, stare into the lens and sniff.

Her Love is a Red Rose

I didn't *see it* see it
but I felt it for weeks,

used it to remember
how much I love you.

A woman, full sari,
running to a Londis,

a crowd of smoked
bees scrambling into

the cracks between
the buildings.

You just never know
these days do you?

What a man is capable of:
a special brew,

a jugular tonk,
a table leg snapped,

a thousand little shards
falling into line.

There is nothing
we can do but

throw our hands
in our jacket pockets,

shout at a volume
nobody hears,

because playing dead
is like romance,

quiet lights, tongues
lowered in reassurance.

The clap of
a shutter down

sets pigeons
into victory salutes.

The woman is
a shook tree

but I do not call
the police.

I'm determined
to make this a love poem.

Now my darling,
I need you to tell me

there was nothing
I could have done.

Mouse

Some like it slow

                    catch 'em by the belly fat

    panic stricken

scarpering themselves to death

        others go for the traps that crack

a head so hard the tail

      shucks turgid from the shock

          find a creature working late

  smash it till it speaks

     a single word of English.

Take this bag of poison.

    A man at the homecoming of British soldiers

        spots a group of protesters shouting

           murderers!

            ingests it

scurries into dinner

     you won't believe what I saw today

    something won't come out

down the pub

    heavy as brick

finds his body stumbling

so mad the bar girl says *closing time*

in open time

when he turns up

at the house of a random *Muzzie*

he doesn't expect

to set the car on fire

it gets in the body

the police barely hold him.

After he's gone

the poison lingers

over everything

he touched

a stench

the wife and kid barely notice

in the clothes

floorboards, letters

a kind of poison of its own

a teenager

sticking a flaming bottle

into the back seat of a car.

everything we used to love
is a Tesco Express

last night a lady asked
about our country
and we felt like crying

progress is a plastic
landmass as big as
America forever
growing in the Atlantic

this is not a drill
everything is changing
faster than you
can die sometimes

we hold so firm
our fingers bleach white
like coral after
the fish have left

Minutes After the Attack

Darkest with curtains just closed, each window sealed,
the street mumbles like a person in the boot of a car.

So dark I lose my hands, stumble to the bathroom,
remove my clothes like I do when a doctor

wants to take a closer look, laying my slabs one by
one on the bathroom floor till they're camouflaged

by *nothing happened.* I forget who I am, girl, boy,
hunk of monkey meat hanging in the emptiness.

Please stop me, I mustn't cry or laugh or want
my mother to hold me, to find me appearing

like the stomach of a cow drifting down a river.

Way Back

when lives were simpler
                              when a child never minded being
called darkie
                    was why no one saw colour
                                                        was why everyone
was the same
                    and that was how it was
                                                        you were one of us

so you should be thankful
                                        was why a father punched a son
for sleeping with a wog
                                was why syphilis fondled the town
was how a chair nutmegged a window
                                                was nothing but blacks
being blacks
                    was when everyone knew everyone
                                                        was why a Pole
who slept with every man at the factory was
                                                            invisible
at church, on road, at the shop

hunky dory
                    you know how
the man down the street
                    was the man at the butcher's
was the man who refused
                    to serve the paki
                              it was ok
                                   freedom
of speech
          was boys being boys
                              brown being black
powdering their bruises
                    everything was peaceful
no one was bothered where you came from
                              just as long as you kept
your head down
          was why we preferred it when the end of the street
was the end of the world
                    back when the end of the world
was for pocketing shells and ornaments and the *other*
                              was why we needed
to lay a table in the centre of the street
                              was why a row of tiny flags
was something to be proud of

Ways of Being Heard

I did what anyone would. Marched until my throat ached,
until I realised violence was the language of negotiation.

What choice do we have when our voices are quieter than
Britney Spears walking her dog up the Strand?

Can't you see the poetry in throwing a fire extinguisher
through the window of the Ritz? Mindless, they said;

but the city can burn so beautifully loud if you let it.
You ever had a shopkeeper grip you like Gatorade?

Tell you to empty your pockets? I was only 14.
I opened my mouth to shout but soil came spilling out,

piano-black from every orifice. There's no use crying.
Some things are hard to say. Here's a flip book of words:

anarchists, fairies, woke militants, Tories... does it hurt yet?
Next time in the shop I pocket a handful of bonbons,

fork tuna behind the birthday cards. *Thugs, hoodlums,*
yobs, scum. A man is on a march in Rotherham,

tells me being labelled *Nazi* hurts like hot poker.
All that soil in his oesophagus. He reaches his hand out

(it's not what he believes; it's what he knows will hurt),
clamps his fingertips together, stretches them toward the sun.

I was just LIVE-fed two young men knife-fighting in Greenwich

handheld and splendidly candid. That's why I love Jackie Chan:
always did his own stunts. To try to forget it I take a bath,

stare at the water, daydream a waterfall of sun-glazed machetes.
Who doesn't, eh? On a balcony a boy asked, *what's happening?*

and someone said *nothing* but meant everything. *Good baths
are a rigmarole*, my bro says. Oils, Epsom salts, whale music.

Everything is happening everywhere in the palm of my hand.
I consider the bathwater violence, as you do, watch it fill to

the absolute lip, lower my foot in, water so scaldingly hot
it feels good, could be the new norm, climbing creepily,

every ligament, huddled amongst bubbles so damn cliquey
all of them two-kissing like rich people, before I know it,

the bath is overflowing and I am swinging my hands like
I'm landing a plane or a plane is landing on my tidy existence.

In the '50s they thought they'd shock sanity back to the body
by dropping a person like a bar of soap into a boiling hot bath.

Thaipusam

Each year, on Archway Road, Hindu devotees prick
their bodies with pins, vows nailed in their cheeks,
swords piercing the flesh between organ and skin.
A local man calls them a bunch of crazy fanatics
but will later drink his liver black till he stumbles
the road, insides splashing Pollock on the asphalt.
Here in the council meeting, it's up-down hysteria,
Whac-A-Mole, each of us a little angrier than last time,
wanting everyone to know what it means to carry
this skin around like a father's ugly coat. We gather
in the road, a crowd of us nailing chorus to the wind.
We want them to know how coarse our insides are,
how hungry we are for someone to hear us, to take
a pin and slowly insert it into our eyelid so we can say,
yes, yes, that is exactly how it feels.

Tank

WARNING VERY GRAPHIC
Islamic State (ISIS) runs over Syrian man with a tank, crushing his
head like a prune

Soon after we check our limbs are still attached,
we watch a man driven over by a tank and wonder
how it feels to have your body crushed so slowly

you hear each bone shift in the skin like peeling white
tape from the pavement.
                            When would you black out?

At kneecap, groin, heart, the lip of the wheels,
caterpillar nonchalant over the tip of your chin like
the feeling of a tumour growing at an alarming rate?

Incidentally, a tumour is growing at an alarming rate.
You thought it was a way away
                            for someone else

but these things get in the lymphs

                                             start running

into schools and the teacher rings a special alarm

so the children dive, trembling, under their desks.
We've mastered the art of imagining our deaths.
We hire camera crews to help us do it

                                                 lining up

the cement blocks,
placing our heads between our knees and

The Expendables

When I remember my father hugging me,
it isn't actually my father hugging me;
it's a movie I saw with Sylvester Stallone.
He's ruffling my hair, launching me up,
telling me not to do something. When I quit
heroin, I didn't exactly quit heroin, more like
saving a seat with a bag down, slipping in
every now and then — methadone, spirits,
TV dinners, YouTube rabbit holes.
My counsellor says I need a new network.
I tell her I have two kids who ignore me —
what else does a man want? Ha ha ha.
I found a flyer, in the margin ads,
some hall in some pebbledash town,
a group of men, some kinda nice,
kinda charming, like this older guy,
buys me a pint, ready salted crisps,
rests his arm on my shoulder,
tells me about last night, after the pub,

they drove the streets till early hours,
spotted a Sikh boy with a local girl,
broke the kid's collar bone. It's just
good to feel part of something.

Don't take this the wrong way but

every time I say *white people* someone tells me
it should be people one said *what you're trying to say*
is that we're all the same ~~white~~ people I don't want
to be making a big brown-arsed scene sometimes
all I want is to forget to curl up to watch a film
where the brown guy is a terrorist and the black girl
dies too quickly to remember her name in another skin
I would have been a nature poet writing about horses
and ladybirds big anecdotes about being a falconer
and that gentleman wouldn't have battered
my eyelid everything would be blissful as it is
outside right now just like when you leave the rave
and the sun's up and it's quiet except for that ringing
he didn't bother me that constant ringing.

If You Don't Like It, Leave

Busloads of far-right demonstrators are feared to be planning to travel hundreds of miles to "defend" memorials at the weekend.
Dan Sabbagh, THE GUARDIAN

I beat myself up a few times a day — not hard enough to leave marks
(as I don't like the questions) but hard enough to feel like a floor

after a party, kissing a lit cig like a fuse from a stick of dynamite.
People ask me why I do it. I tell them when I put my feet up

I imagine a dumbbell landing on my kneecap, leg twisting, crack
in on itself. What makes you feel at home more than your local?

What makes you fight more than the people you love? We on a bus,
a community heading to the big smoke, placards on laps,

old songs, Madness. I'm not a fan of places I don't know
so when the fight breaks out, I do what anyone would.

There's a freedom in the feeling of a fist through the film of an eye,
flooding to the whites of a sclera, till it shines like a bloody medal.

the city hums
like a closed cafe's
fish tank
moss heavy
enough
to lose sight
of your own
shaking hands

on nights like this
we men
either push it in
or punch it out
it's something
to feel
the light
sending darkness
downward dogging
up the patio

human nature
has a knack
for the inhumane
must have slipped
our minds to hear
a child slamming
on the glass

most nights we tell
our daughters
there is something
in our eyes
when it is in fact
the knowledge
that we have
the potential
to do something
they can never find out

I Love You Man

There is always so much violence when we are together
because there is so much togetherness after the violence.

In the pink of victory, our wounds make eyes in the dark,
eyes find podiums in our mouths, scars write bios on our bodies;

look at him lick the laughter from my cuts, tails of anthems
belted out in the sombre streets of 3am, a snap at a bollard,

a woman runs scared, a curtain snatched, a bus stop: shrapnel.
There is so much hope in togetherness, in stringing voices up,

swinging fists high enough to punch the moon from the sky.
We smoke on a stoop on the slabs of my dad's old market stall.

He wants to thank me for kicking that kid so hard he didn't kick back
but settles for calling me a crazy fucker. It's nothing, I say.

I love you like the weight of my boot in the face of that cunt.
There is always so much love when we are together.

Youtube.com/watch?v=MkqLs6ZX_TQ
(Please do not watch this)

a clip
fell out or

in me
this morning

cop a feel
full of ENTER

an mpeg can be
a vehicle for

revenge I mean
social change

I mean why not
post a post

aching with
shock watch it

played like
a cheap stripper

look at this scum
a picture can

be the sharp point
of a thousand

words and like
like like like

a flock of pheasants
after the pans

and pots clatter
let's make sure

everyone knows
who this sicko is

drop her
beanbag

clunk
a woman will be

too scared
to leave her home

something will be
scrolled on her wall

she will have
to be let go

in a year she will
do something

she'll regret

While Trying the Crème Brûlée

My uncle joined the Tamil Tigers because he wanted to be an actor.
His father wouldn't allow it. The acting, I mean. Uncle ran bag-handed,
snuck loose in a clapped-out truck. Dumb enough to want a gun,
young enough not to know where to point it. Today at dinner, we go
from cricket to bomb shelter, uncover a dimple in a shoulder blade,
the tale of a bullet that made itself at home, now banter for airport staff,
keepsake, memento, something to squeeze and laugh, to remind him
of his late friend who used to roll cigs in bread paper. Big as a building,
neither low nor fast enough and too heavy to carry, he left him there.
Watched him for hours or days through a crack in a wall, breaking.
The body jerked like it was remembering what it wanted to say.
When my uncle returned to tell the family, he didn't speak a word;
the mother fell slack as if someone had pulled away her spine.
My uncle on the doorstep, silently squeezing his shoulder to tears.

Nothing British

about
a sister

tossed from
a car at 5am

nothing routine
about spring

appearing all
over her body

a mother
blowing fear

into a brown
paper bag

that night
a boy presses

an ear to
a beaker

a beaker to
a bedroom door

memorises
the sound

of a father
catching

resentment
in the hook

of his elbow
this will be

the tale
he clings to

the crux
he grips

humiliation
can be an

heirloom
shiny in

the basement
he and two friends

have had it
up to here

The Man Who Played Records to Aliens

You can find him shacked up in electronic bric-a-brac,
a wonderfully phallic family of blip blopping knobs,
tubes tonguing cathodes oscillating line dot line
below a bromance of winking lights and LED disco balls.
In the garden, a two-storey, 150,000 volt satellite
balanced on a dismantled ski lift, a tractor's wheel arch,
a bath rail from a dead mother's bath. All bent out,
then into shape in a life's work: an alien boombox.
Every afternoon, morning, middle of the night,
Led Zeppelin, Sun Ra, Coltrane blaring into the ether.
What else can a man do but raid another car boot,
reach beyond the tiny town where he was raised,
the same town where another man around the same age
builds a shed to house his Nazi memorabilia.

The Calling

Just got word that will shock the world – Land of the free...
home of the brave DAMN PROUD TO BE AN AMERICAN!
@therock

At school a boy just kicked a chair so hard it bent over like it was searching for a contact lens. *Just another day at college*, says the teacher, two months from retirement. *We've built a breakout space, they need to know violence won't be tolerated.* The boy holds his temper like a trophy, reupholstering a set of lines from *The Godfather: deep breaths, deep breaths.* What do a teacher from Highgate, a soldier in Afghanistan and a boy from Tower Hamlets have in common? On this day, five years ago, President Obama announced the death of Osama Bin Laden; but it was actually Dwayne 'The Rock' Johnson who announced the death. To celebrate the end of term they watch a movie where a terrorist is shot in the face, someone shouts *this is racist* and everybody laughs. When a girl insults a boy's personal hygiene, the boy shrinks like bad fondant and it's not unexpected to see it curtail into a type of snuff where the same boy, frothing like wild boar, makes bloody half-moons down the neck of another. The breakout space is filled with newspapers, whale noises and low lights. In *The Economist* a British soldier with PTSD describes normal life as a breakout space from duty. It must be three weeks later, four broken chairs, one fractured wrist, Careers Day. A soldier served twice in Afghanistan. The teacher says, *this could be your calling.* The soldier asks, *are you a fan of war films?* The soldier's uniform is pristinely ironed, boots shiny, hat straight as a landing site. The boy is so excited about being part of a team on patrol. A dilapidated house, a routine stop, a child appearing out of nowhere, drops in a bundle. The teacher is refurnishing his flat in Highgate.

maybe we focus
on the whale when
really it is the ocean
that led us here

that inconceivable
counterbalance
shrugging like
coincidence
convincing a boat
to split and a man
to float like an arm
surfing the wind
from a car window

notice how the flipper
lands a spray
like bus stop
the people gasp

reminded
that maniacs
are light relief
after we leave
the ocean is undeterred
a light touch
below the elbow

This Is Not an IED

after Danez Smith

it's a list poem
a suspicious looking package in the back seat of a van
a disembodied window
a market stall melting
a car dressed as an autumn tree
your vocal cords
cranked tight as wrists
jumping at the scream of a siren
the exhaustion of trying to explain
this isn't an IED, this is a poem
about being pulled from your home at 4am
neighbours poking through curtains
a bedroom left sideways
a stamped body in a white van
let's start from the beginning
bed, Bible, TV, commode, lamp
broken finger, sprained ankle
a son gathers the pieces of a father

who isn't really his father
doesn't really laugh like his father
this isn't an IED
it's a son throwing a fist through a door
placing a poem in a duffle bag
leaving the bag in a white van
in the busiest part of the city

Hate

I lower the window, a drunk shouts, *what is it about hate that you love so much?* and I say, *sorry mate I don't*

— have the faintest what he means so I chase him to a church where the pavement is lined with spikes.

Free acupuncture, the man shouts and every part of me prickles. He tells me how he loved his girlfriend

so much he put a baseball bat through her head, *ever love something so much you can't let it go?* I shut my

eyes Christmas Eve-tight. Imagine all the things I've ever known disintegrating. On the radio, a mother,

married 33 years, killed by her husband for proclaiming her sexuality; a Traveller forced into a flat pokes

hot ash through his own letterbox. Love can be a kindling, can be the perfect feast for a bunch of Venn diagrams walking into a bar, one says to the other, *it wasn't like this before*, and everyone is

swinging their shoulders, code words for *I miss it when*. I'm telling you this because I want to prepare

you before you see it: a love crime, a sister raped, a brother, the wrong assailant, a head hugged

by a car door. It feels ok to fill the void with bits of a forehead: *have you ever loved someone, like really loved them?*

Mortal Kombat

There's a hell of a lot of blood gushing from an open neck.
I cannot believe how my nephews huddle round a TV shouting

Finish Him. Pixels dandelion from the top of a spine,
so realistic you can almost feel it running between the synapses.

Thing about real life is: a head rarely comes clean off in a single strike.
It requires a sharp saw through the arch of the spinal column, back and

all that hilarity, forth, until a head sees the body it came from.
Imagine seeing the body you came from for a whole seven seconds.

Somewhere someone is kicked to their knees. Somewhere someone
is figuring the best angle to film it. The machete winks at the sun.

My nephews are elated. A Chinese man has been cut into tiny pieces.
Here's a thought: following the making of *Mortal Kombat 11*,

developers were diagnosed with PTSD. Here's another. In Dursley
a boy recreates *Mortal Kombat* executions on a mannequin stolen

from Debenhams. *You walk around the office*, a game designer said,
one guy's studying hangings, the other's watching a kid's guts fall out.

Somewhere someone is researching the best way to kill a journalist.
I urge you not to watch a man decapitated. Not all it's cracked up to be,

though it was the second most popular video after the Britain's
Got Talent dance sequence. My nephew shouts, *FINISH HIM*,

leaping off the couch to karate chop a schoolfriend dead.
All that blood, imagine it, flickering across the carpet.

PREVENT

The CCTV is a raised eyebrow outside a block of flats
capturing something indecipherable, call it a haggis —

sheep's pluck encased in our stomach lining — call it
a myth, whim; call it an anti-extremist's fantasy.

Let's begin a haggis hunt. It's a wonderful game starting
with a taster of haggis, let it roll clumsy in the mouth

like a man shouting *Allahu Akbar* a little too loudly.
Enough to throw everyone out banging pots and pans,

attaching bumper stickers, flags, black bags to windows.
It's all part of the show; before you know it the group

cracks, splinters into two gangs. Some are wild haggis
dressed in exotic clothes and inappropriate headwear;

others are haggis-hunters, dressed in perhaps the same.
And so it begins, the chase; hunters smash giant chess

pieces through backdoors, twisting wrists up the smalls
of backs, relentless as a pair of binoculars balanced

on a fence, a bug to the backseat, a bundle of
wires stripping your chest hair, *you scratch my back —*

all day, eyes up, eyes down, soft powers on soft targets,
everything for your own good. Yesterday a Somali man

was turned inside out; his flat was no smoke without fire.
If you have any info on the whereabouts of the haggis

it's your chance to speak, but he doesn't say a thing. After
the raid he presses a cup to the collective chest of the block

and hears the song of an open wound, flowering.

Einstein said

the total amount of energy in existence has always been
the total amount of energy in existence. that is to say

some words, I'd rather not repeat, stick in the hinges,
cajoled like bunting after a hurricane.

That is to ask the question: where does all that energy go?
We'll be back after this short message.

Somewhere in America, scientists waft perfume in a tank,
an aroma similar to almonds and cherries, watch closely

as an electric current shoots through a rodent's legs.
Every time it breathes that scent it feels the jolt pulse;

bones knock so it jumps like it is remembering a world
without cherries and almonds and torture and slowly

the scent becomes the current becomes a terror, guttural,
packing a rodent into a tiny ball in the corner of the tank.

I can't get it out, sat here, the same seat, the same 472 bus,
just in front of another white woman, no relation at all,

who doesn't say something I'd rather not repeat,
but I recoil, curl so my spine juts spikes up my back,

my daughter beside me, blowing hot air onto the window,
fingering tiny tally marks just to watch them disappear.

Apparently the rodent would bash its face against the tank
until the pulse shocked him to death. Wait, there's more:

a generation on, the rodent's grandson in a different tank,
completely unaware of the suffering of its forefathers,

woken terrified at the scent of almonds and cherries.
My daughter is asking me why we got off the bus early.

have you ever seen
the sea leave
its ocean
or a country
leave its border

or an anger
leave a body
bloody on
the road

have you ever
held an axe
and dreamed
of a head it
could fall into
somewhere

something
is snatching

at a hook
somehow
all of us are
wishing we
weren't so
easily pulled
by a current

like skin
crawling between
the buildings

Suspicious-looking Individual

All soldiers should die and go to hell. The lowlife fucking scum.
Azhar Ahmed, 20

While you are reading this someone is reading you *fuck all British values*. You really shouldn't have read that. You're red-flagged and a MI5 newbie is calling his boss, a boss is calling his wife, a wife is calling her secret lover for an hour of horny sex. This is escalation. Just this morning you spoke to an extremist next door — *how was your weekend?* — enough to shift you from moderate to alarming, alerting a crack team while the boss's wife takes it doggy over a kitchen counter. That's extreme. Everyone is staring at you drinking coffee at a known terror hotspot (they have an Italian coffee machine). Your text reads, *I gotta stay strong for these infidels.* It's racy enough to rustle the leaves of the newbie, the boss and a SWAT team, all of them crammed in a DHL truck eating Krispy Kreme, taking pictures of you, when really the boss is texting his wife, *sorry I'm working late.* You really shouldn't have bought that tape and Polyfilla for the bathroom, nor bumbled around in a sarong after prayers. That afternoon, you're on the extremist hotlist. You're wanted. A threat to national security. And the boss just got a text from his wife saying, *that was ducking hot*, which incites the order

to raid and sure enough they blaze through a door, pull a man from
his bed, stuff a pair of stockings in his mouth while his wife shouts,
it's not how it looks.

44 Ways to Make and Kill a Terrorist

It isn't easy asking questions to a dead man,
what with all the blood, the right arm slumped

like a newborn's neck. I thank him for coming
so soon after the drone strike. *History*, he says,

favours the living, but today he wants to tell me
how it feels to have a story disembodied.

But first, here are the things he shows me:
a family photo burnt black; a speech redacted;

protest pamphlets; *Battle For Peace* Issue 86.
I can hardly make out his words, his cheek

full of nail bomb, but he takes my hand,
presses his thumb to the centre of my palm

and describes olive trees, old as grandmothers,
in the field outside his home, never touched,

nor carved on by lovers or kissed by travellers.
It's the soil, he says. *This country is coarse with terror,*

landmines like IOUs from soldiers who poked
peepholes in our bodies, hid triggers in our roots.

He squeezes white in the middle of my palm
like the glowing smudge on a pilot's monitor.

When it hit, he says, *I was blown amongst the trees,*
beneath the black branches trying to catch the sky

and my boy, white with silt, I could see him,
he would not turn away, he could not hear me

shouting, please no, don't look for me here,
like my forefathers shouted to their children

because it isn't easy asking questions to a dead man.

House, Bus Stop, Bus, Driver

My baby girl sits so squeaky clean,
organs rubbing up on each other
like balloons in a telephone booth.
She loves to point: *house, lady, car.*
She really is perfect in the sense

she's not broken yet. That's why
we stare, sigh, coo. Yesterday:
city, building, postbox, scooter.
A woman said she was the most
beautiful baby she had ever seen.

Today one asked if we wondered
what colour she would pop out:
hand, knuckle, finger, nail.
I know she doesn't understand me:
police, siren, truncheon. But it's scary

how quickly she picks things up.
At the park a boy snatches her blankie

so she slams him to the ground.
That's wrong, I tell her, *don't do that*,
while patting her softly on the back.

True Lies

My bro's so good at dying, he shakes this way and that,
dancing in the shrapnel. Mama shouts, *play nice*, so
we bundle into the sofa bed, bodies clumsily naive.

Arnie's on the telly, a CIA agent, a body of nothing but
muscle and man, chasing a terrorist (I forget his name),
trying to stop him nuking the world, stealing $60 million,

it doesn't matter, because Arnie throws a knife so hard
the handle juts from the eye like a lever on a ghost train.
Good ol' Arnie; he'd make a shoot-out funny, a sex scene

violent, a string of dead bodies entertaining. *You're fired!*
They're all bad guys after all, with coughed-up names,
indecipherable lines, from countries too terrible to visit.

That's the beauty of a blockbuster; it can take you anywhere.
25 years later, Arnie's a politician, my bro and I on the bus,
a man in full thobe walks on. The thought rolls in like a tank.

Salad

My Aunty cuts the cucumbers slender as the tissue on the inside
        of a cheek.
If you're going to go, she tells me, *wouldn't you rather go in style —*
        a firework,

an explosion, a man setting himself on fire outside the Parliament.
He made his dying into a kind of bouquet.

No one wants to go without a fight, backed into a corner.
It's a matter of considering the options, she says, scraping in the tomato.

Who to call, where to go, how it feels pressed snug to a breast;
the supermarket, the approximate distance from the entrance to the aisle

where the eggs meet the bread counter, how a button feels below
the weight of a thumb. *We interrupt this broadcast to bring you —*

My family seated for lunch, Aunty laughing about the buttering
        of my bread.
It feels like I am seeing her for the very first time.

A Decent Pair of Nikes

You ever clucked for hate? Ramshackled the sofa for it?
Imagined the whole street a bag full of cracked glass?

Sometimes you hear a war reporter reporting war and it feels
like a dealer texting you to say he's got something nice.

Have a gander at this: a mother tries to scream her son to life,
an arm hung as overdose, a baby caked in loss. Stick

a handful of these Polaroids to the insides of your head.
Sirens? Hardly notice them, hardly news, hardly truth,

hardly something to write home about. Skip forward a bit:
my mother tells me that during the war in Sri Lanka you could

have a man killed for £90. Imagine dying for the price
of these Nikes; imagine a field full of old Nikes, footless,

hanging from a line, a shoelace here, a tongue loose there.
See how we've made ourselves at home, barricaded in,

swimming in the flesh, smoke like air, fisting like kissing.
Two missiles draw parking spaces in the sky. When the man

appears in the clip, waving a meat cleaver around a church,
it is actually a man wanting a life worth more than £90;

it is actually the sun reverse-parking in the sky. Look closely:
a pair of Nikes peeking below a flag. Watch carefully

how he grips his chest like his heart is reaching from his body,
as if it's finally found the will to walk.

we will not feel different
or be able to notice
the way we hardly spot
summer end and winter
wet behind the ears
is in the guts yelling
stare at a TV close enough
you will only make out
the pixels like plankton
gasping in the panic
searchlights combing
the sea bed calling
for a time we could see
ourselves in ourselves

the city is the bends
everywhere is dolphin
mistaken for whale
a mother watches
her goldfish repeatedly

smash into a window
maybe this is what
beginnings sound like
the hiss of white noise
the faint edge of an 'e'
blooming into the music
of a thousand machetes

A Cigarette Tastes Better When the House is Full

To say a tree begins at the bark
is like saying a killer
begins at the killing.

My girlfriend says
I need to work
on my dinner party chat.

Keep it light.

Over the ratatouille
a gardener tells me,

to stop the roots raising the pavement
the council trim the tips of the branches.

Some facts
are better stories.

It takes dessert
for someone to be reminded
of the man murdered by police.

They thought he was a terrorist
but it turns out
there was something
in his eyes.

Everyone is shaking their heads
before wishing they smoked.

Outside I lose a staring match with the moon.
The road is a spinal cord,
the trees, severed nerve endings.

Days Before

Nobody sleeps anymore.
We press shoulders to beds, and
wait like you do for bad news.
In a few pages something
regrettable will happen.
I'm not talking about a drain
taking a bite out of a floorboard,
a woman calling a handyman
who says he'll be over tomorrow;
he won't be over tomorrow
because a young policeman
has been promoted to sergeant.
Since promotion he wonders
why he feels so full of man.
He fucks so surprisingly well,
his lover asks breathlessly,
where did that come from?
He hasn't the faintest and
neither does the handyman
who will gush all over his shirt.

Something is about to happen.
A body will sound like a whale
dropped from a high rise.
In a few days the woman
will be shocked. *He was just here,*
she'll say. *He was stood right there.*

Magic Eye

Start with the tip of your nose against the centre of the picture;
recoil slowly. You are discovering something astounding, easy.
Let the brain lather, a bubble bath of pixels, a clumsy-headed gasp

at shape. Don't panic; the answers are always in the back of the book
like *bridge, corner shop, cracked wing mirror, radio*. Back to the image.
Can you see it? they'll ask, *reaching from stone, there, a whale flailing*.

You can pretend even if you can't as no one wants to feel left out,
but finally, on Platform 3, a fleshy mess, in the butt of a full stop,
you see it now, right there, in the blur, appearing as easy as a story.

A Year On

An investigation will be rolled out
as far as the veins can reach

as far as the knuckles will drag
letters of support drowning until

letters of condolence drip dry until
nothing but *oh I think I remember*

nothing but an independent inquiry
tracing fragments of bullet in body

fragments of bodies in bullets
distraction is a wonderful thing

wonder is a distracting thing
a policeman exits stage right

it isn't easy to keep our hands high
with so much horror to point at

a policeman enters stage left
easier to forget what it is to be

a mother gaunt as autumn
an enquiry like a forest felled

I dreamt of a word yesterday
something heavier than failure

bigger than *deepest regret*
something to describe how it is

to be the killer and the victim
fighting in the belly of a whale.

Objects Increase Their Distance at Ever-increasing Speeds

In 22 billion years   there is a strong possibility   that the
universe   will expand   so severely   that everything

will be pulled from itself   stars   from their galaxies,
atoms   from their molecules,   limbs from their sinews

until   the very   fabric   of   space   and time
the pixels   out   of   wh i c h   our   univ   erse is co

nst   ruc t e   d w   ill   begin   to   se   par   ate   and   rip
In 22 minutes, a big bang of bodies, an orgasm let loose from the

stable, sweethearts since school fold as bad origami around two
singing blue stripes straight as horizon, she falls into his shoulder

whispers *we're going to have a* — universe is growing in her tummy,
desire lines through the house, look how they make the time and

energy and space reimagining their existence, adoration in every
particle of their being, first steps, first school, first love, first stop

and search, a patrol officer on his first day on duty, imagines that
22-year-old face as someone else's face, reimagines a leather tool

belt as a suicide vest, running for the Tube as running from police
and listen the universe is beginning to stretch taut, five bodies

like dead horses pile on the man's back, nine bullets through
his head, one   is enough   to   rip   every thing   apart, it

isn't   pretty   in a semi   detached in   Tower   Hamlets
a phone   pulled   from a   palm, a mother   stripped

from her   words,   a universe wrenched   from a gut.
Every   particle   in her body   s ev   ered e very a tom

h   ollowed   into n   oth   ing, t he em   ptiness can b e de
afening b a   bb   ling   in   a   lan   gua ge   no   one

un   derstands   yo   u can   not reco   gnise t he mot   her
af ter   the   uni   verse is rip   ped   to   smit   here   ens, what

is th   ere   but   t   he spa   ce   wh ere h er   son
once   l i   ved   t   h   e   em   pty   ch   a   ir.

Arji Manuelpillai | 103

ACKNOWLEDGEMENTS

From the initial idea to the final product this book has been a collaborative process made possible through the love and support from so many wonderful writers.

Firstly, I need to say thank you to Hannah Lowe, my mentor, who has continued to be a great source of inspiration throughout my writing life. I need to also show gratitude to 'Feedbachus' – that's Maia Elsner, April Yee and Jessica Murrain – who helped me with the final stages. Thanks also to other writers including Wayne Holloway-Smith, Anthony Anaxagorou, Emma Jeremy, Will Gee, Alice Hiller, Cecilia Knapp, Sophia Nicholson and all of Stanza and Malika's Poetry Kitchen family.

Also thanks to Arts Council England for their financial support and the Jerwood/Arvon Mentoring Programme for their faith in me. A special high five to my friend Lauren Irving; without her I would not have got the funding.

I'd love to take the time to thank all the interviewees who gave me invaluable insight into understanding hate crime and extremism. This includes Ivan Humble, Professor Hilary Pilkington, Vidyan Ravinthiran, Nicola Benyahia and Kannan Vasuthevan. I should also include those anonymous names who offered advice and assistance by phone, in real life and on Zoom. It could have been a chat in a rally, in a protest march, or simply a discussion at the pub. I appreciate you all.

On top of this I had great help from a number of powerful books. These included: *The Muslims are Coming: Islamophobia, Extremism, and the Domestic War on Terror* by Arun Kundnani, *The Cambridge Companion to Religion and Terrorism* edited by James R. Lewis, *Explaining Terrorism* by Martha Crenshaw, *Loud and Proud* by Hilary Pilkington, *Understanding Hate Crimes* by Carolyn Turpin-Petrosino, the research gathered in www.dare-h2020.org, *Soft Targets* by Deborah Landau, the work of J. Levin & McDevitt and *The Islamist* by Ed Husain.

Finally, I have to thank my family for their continued belief. Appa and Mama and all my brothers. My partner Anna Bruder, her mum Maggie Bruder, and finally my daughter Aarabi. May you sow only good things in this Earth.

Versions of these poems appeared in *Finished Creatures, Ink Sweat and Tears, bath magg, The Poetry Review, Poetry Wales* and *The North*.